An Elementary Author Guide To -- Metadata

Adam Cartwright

Anickto Publishing

Anickto Publishing

(www.anickto.com)

Copyright © 2025 Adam Cartwright

All rights reserved.

The right of Adam Cartwright to be identified as the author of this work has been asserted by him in accordance with the Copyright, Designs and Patents Act 1988.

No part of this publication may be reproduced, stored in a retrieval system, or transmitted, in any form or by any means without prior written permission of the publisher, nor be otherwise circulated in any form of binding or cover other than that in which it is published and without a similar condition being imposed on the subsequent purchaser.

paperback ISBN 978-1-7385435-8-8

eBook ISBN 978-1-7385435-9-5

Cover Design by Adam Cartwright

Contents

Introduction	V
How to Use this Guide	VII
1. Metadata	1
2. Title	7
3. ISBNs	13
4. Category	19
5. Genre	29
6. Keywords	37
7. Blurb	43
8. Age & Grade	53
9. Contributors	57
10. Copyright	63
11. Price	71
12. Author Bio	77
Metadata Checklist	81

About the Author	85
Also by Adam Cartwright	87
Acronyms	89
Index	91

INTRODUCTION

With this series of Elementary Author Guides, my intention is to do exactly as the title implies: provide you with an easy to follow, straightforward, step-by-step process for getting your book off the ground. There are many far more detailed guides available in both book and digital formats. I make no pretence at competing with them. My only aim is to try to make things as simple as I can for you by limiting content to the fundamentals of book writing and publishing.

Metadata is important for your book. It provides information, which is used by the book industry as a whole, book retailers, libraries, and readers. Without metadata, it'll be as if your book doesn't exist. In this guide, you'll find an explanation of metadata and the various components that form it. To help you make the most of the opportunities metadata offers, I've added chapters which explain, in a step-by-step manner, how you find, develop, collate, and enter appropriate details. You won't find chapters for every element because some are self-explanatory. I've only added information that I think will help you.

You should be aware, I'm not claiming to be an expert. I have no formal training or any academic qualifications in any of the authoring, book writing, or book publishing disciplines. What I share with you comes from my experience as a ghostwriter, from assisting others with their book development, and from research.

Adam Cartwright

How to Use this Guide

Start by reading chapter 1 'Metadata'. This provides you with an overview and some basic information. Thereafter, it's up to you.

If you've not had anything to do with metadata before, I suggest you read through the chapters in the order presented. Please note, though I've tried to follow a logical sequence, there's no right or wrong order. Different systems ask for the information in varying order.

If you already have some knowledge, and understand some aspects, you're free to jump to whichever chapter interests you.

If you're interested in a specific topic but can't find it quickly, go to the Index toward the end of this book.

I've added a brief resume of each chapter's content at its end under 'Takeaway'. You can use this to see if the chapter is of any interest to you.

1

METADATA

You'll see metadata described in various terms, such as data about data, a set of data that describes and gives information about other data, an underlying definition or description, and more.

The word 'meta' comes from the Greek for 'after', 'beyond', but is now primarily recognised as meaning 'about', as you may see from the descriptions in the first paragraph above.

Metadata, in one form or another, has always existed, though the term did not come into general use until the 1960s. Beforehand, it would have been termed something like a record, an index, a listing, a catalogue, or similar. For example, before computerisation, libraries used card indexes to record details of all the books held.

Principally, metadata is information created and stored during the creation of a book or product. Metadata doesn't just apply to books.

Because this is a guide for book metadata, I'll centre in on books. However, many of the points will also apply to other product types.

Ask yourself, 'How will readers find my book?'. Think of the various answers you come up with. You can usually find most of them, in one format or another, within the metadata. That's why you should spend time ensuring yours is as clear and easy to understand as possible. You want people to buy your book, so do all you can to help them.

When considering book metadata, you'll probably first think of title, sub-title, author, and cover. Those are the basic metadata components. There are, however, many more parts. Don't let the length of the following list put you off. It's not as hard to handle as it looks. I've given brief explanations against several. The others are self-explanatory. Where I think it'll help, I've written a detailed explanation of the topic in a separate chapter. You can find these from either the contents list at the front or from the Index at the back.

Note: The order of chapters does not imply priority or preference. All parts of your metadata are important.

- Title (and sub-title);

- ISBN (International Standard Book Number);

- Category (either the BISAC (Book Industry Standards and Communications) code, Thema codes, or category choice entered in retailers like Amazon.);

- Genre (e.g. Thriller, Romance, Memoir, etc.);

- Keywords (A word, combination of words, or short phrase describing the book);

- Blurb (The book description you include on back covers and online book pages.);

- Age & Grade range;

- Contributors (Those who've been involved with creating your book.);

- Copyright;

- Price;

- Author biography. (A brief insight into who you are.);

- Series (if applicable);

- Publication date;

- Format (Hardback, Paperback, Ebook, Audiobook);

- Trim size (book dimensions e.g. 5.25 x 8.25, 6 x 9, etc.);

- Page count;

- Word count;

- Spine width;

- Weight (Print editions);

- Language;

- Sales territory (e.g. USA, UK, Australia, etc.);

- And More.

As you see, metadata is anything that defines a book, its content, and its availability. I've listed the primary ones, but there are other components that may comprise part of your metadata.

Metadata is pivotal to discoverability (*find, come across, locate, stumble upon, bring to light*) and is used extensively by search engines. It's a crucial element in marketing and sales. Without it, readers are unlikely to come across your book. It will probably just lie dormant in some dark corner (*physical or digital*).

Takeaway

- Metadata comprises all the various bits of relevant and incidental information about your book.

- Good metadata helps readers find your book.

- Without accurate metadata, readers are unlikely to find your book.

- Search engines use metadata to answer readers' questions.

2

Title

The title, along with the cover, is the first impression of your book a reader is likely to receive. There's some debate about which is the more important, title or cover. Most suggest it's the cover because it's a visual image, and society now tends to be more visually centred. In the past, words and phrases bore the most weight. No matter which argument you support, it's undeniable that the title can grab attention.

In the past, popular thought was that a one word title is best. That was prior to the arrival, and wide use, of online search engines. Google, for example. These have changed the ground. A one word search will bring endless lists of results, most of which won't relate to your book. The suggestion is now for authors to consider increasing their book titles to three or four words, a search of which is more likely to return relevant results.

Choosing a title is not as easy as it may sound. There are several factors to consider, besides whether you like what you've come up with. It's difficult to let go of our good ideas, but if we're serious about trying to get our books into readers' hands, we often have to. That working title you've used for so long may prove unsuitable for what you hope to achieve. A 'working title' is the preliminary title we use for drafting our manuscripts.

I'll provide you with a few ideas on how to find your title, but before I do, one warning. It's import for you to find an original title. When you've gained an idea of what you'd like it to be, make sure you do a thorough search. You'll often be surprised to discover that another author is already using the title, or something very similar. I'd suggest searching the internet and book retail sites such as Amazon. Bear in mind, though Amazon is the world's largest online retail site, it doesn't have every book on it.

When thinking of a title, there're a few things you should try to aim for:

- Short.

- Easy to remember.

- Suggestive.

- Memorable.

- Unique.

Though the principles still apply, it may not be easy to achieve this with non-fiction books. These often require a longer title to state clearly the topic under discussion. You should still try to come up with something that catches a reader's initial attention, if you can.

A point someone raised, and one I think is worth bearing in mind, is to try and avoid a title that somehow makes reference to something controversial, unless it's the basis for your book. Any implied connection may cause readers to bypass your book. I appreciate you may think it'll create intrigue, but it can be a dangerous area for you and your book.

Another thing to avoid is the temptation to give your book the same title as a famous or popular book. You may think it'll get more attention. It may, but when readers search it, the famous, popular book will come up first and yours is likely to be buried somewhere in the depths of the internet. How often do you bother to look past the first page of a search result? You may get frustrated with the time and effort it takes, but coming up with a unique title for your book will benefit you.

Now for a few ideas on what could help you find your title.

- Have a look at other books in your genre. There's often a trend that you'd want to adopt in some way, if it fits.

- What about your characters? Is there one whose name would make a good title? The most obvious recent success is Harry Potter. A well-known one from the past is David Copperfield.

- If there's an important setting in your book, try thinking of ways to use that in a title.

- Think about what makes your book different from others in the genre. There may be something there you can use.

Those are just a few ideas. As you see, there are many areas you can look at to find the basis for your book's title. You could also try what's known as 'free writing'. That's where you give your mind free rein and write out whatever comes into it: words, phrases, names, locations, and more. Don't worry about it making sense at this stage. Leave it overnight and when you return, you'll be surprised at how much is usable. You might even find the title for your next book.

Following the above process should help you avoid a title already in use or one similar to it. However, there can be the rare occasion when it may not work. An author I know researched their title, but when they published, they discovered another book with exactly the same title, word for word, had been simultaneously published. It was in a different genre, but when they searched the title, the other book always came up first. In this instance, there'd been no way for my author friend to know. As I said, it's a rare occurrence, but one you should be aware of.

So far, I've not mentioned subtitles. You can use them to add some clarity to your main title. For example, Matthew Perry, the actor from the TV series 'Friends', gave his memoir the primary title of 'Friends, Lovers, and the Big Terrible Thing'. It's a catchy title but doesn't really say what the book is about. To clarify he added, as a subtitle 'A Memoir'. This makes clear to prospective readers what they'll encounter in the book. If possible, without forcing the issue, try to include some relevant keywords[1], but don't overdo it. In Matthew's subtitle, 'Memoir' is a keyword.

Though I've included mention of subtitles in this chapter, they're a separate part of your book's metadata. Make sure, when completing submission forms, you enter it in its own field and don't lump it together with your primary title. That said, there may be occasions when you want the primary title you've identified and the sub-title to be shown together. In that instance, they combined become the primary title. The two parts are usually separated with

---

1. *Keywords are the topic of chapter 6*

a colon (:). You'd then leave the sub-title field in the submission form blank. Remember to always use the same format wherever your book title is to appear.

Note: If you're writing a series, don't include the series name in the subtitle. They've their own metadata field.

Takeaway

- Your book's title should be short, easy to remember, and memorable.

- Use a subtitle if you think you need to add more clarity.

- To assist search results, try having a three or four word title.

- Research your title to ensure it's not already being used.

- Don't use titles from famous or popular books.

3

ISBNs

If you've any interest in books, which I assume you have as you're reading this, you'll undoubtedly have come across some reference to an ISBN. But, what is an ISBN? And what's it all about?

The letters 'ISBN' stand for 'International Standard Book Number'. These are unique identifier codes that are only relevant to 'single' text based (*often referred to as 'monographic'*) publications. This includes books (in all formats), pamphlets, maps, mixed media (*where most of the content is text based*), and more. They can't be used for other text-based items such as magazines, journals, and so on, which do not fall within the single publication definition. *Other products can have unique identifier codes, but those aren't of interest to us here.*

An ISBN identifies a book's: title, edition, publisher, language, originating territory, physical properties (*trim size (height, width, depth), page count, and format (hardback, paperback, ebook, audiobook*)). ISBNs act as global identifiers, which are used in over two hundred countries.

Publishers, bookshops, online retailers, distributors, libraries, universities, academic organisations, and wholesalers use ISBNs. They help them manage all stages of a book's process within their organisations, such as cataloguing, ordering, shelf placing, stock control, sales analysis, and so on.

I'll not take up your time, or mine, to detail the history of ISBNs, but to say they started life in 1965 and came into wide usage in 1970, with the ten number format. The thirteen number format we now know came into use in 2007.

In most countries, there's no legal requirement for a book to have an ISBN. However, there are a few where such a requirement is prescribed by law. There are also some which impose a higher rate of tax on books that don't have an ISBN. Yes, in case you didn't realise, tax is payable on all books.

ISBNs are not free per se, though you'll often see and hear reference to 'free ISBNs'. I'll come to that in a moment. ISBNs have to be bought from an appointed agency. Each country has one that is legally permitted to sell them. In the UK it is Nielsen, in the USA it is R. R. Bowker. A search of the internet for your own country should provide you with details of your appointed agency. ISBNs are country specific and must be purchased from the responsible agency for that country. That will be the country in which you live and write. ISBNs aren't cheap, but as you'll see shortly, are worth the expenditure in some situations.

You're probably now groaning about yet another drain on your meagre finances. There are alternatives. As mentioned earlier, there are such things as 'free ISBNs'. At least they are free to you. Most, though not all, publishing systems that are geared for self-publishing authors offer free ISBNs or, in the case of Amazon, their equivalent of an ASIN (Amazon Standard Identification Number). These'll help you as a self-publishing author get your book published and out into the reading world with little, if any, cost. However, these come with some disadvantages.

A free ISBN or ASIN means the company that gave it to you is identified as the publisher, not you. This also means, if, to give your book the widest possible exposure, you use more than one publishing company, as many of us do, you'll have several different identifiers for the same book. It also means you don't have total control over your book and the various details made available to the public. It's not my intention to worry you or put you off. I know authors who have used free ISBNs and ASINs for years. I'm simply trying to put things in context. To that end, I'll explain the advantages of having your own ISBN.

Before I get to that, here is some guidance to help you decide whether to purchase your own ISBN. You need to determine what your overall aim is. Is the book just for family and friends? Do you want to sell it to the wider reading public? Do you plan on publishing many more books? If your answer to the first is yes, you don't really need to worry about having your own ISBN. If you've answered yes to the other two, it'll be worth considering your own ISBN.

The advantages of having your own ISBN are:

- Bibliographic databases[1] will identify you, or your imprint[2], as the publisher.

- You use the same ISBN no matter how many publishing sites you publish through.

- They provide consistency when publishing several books.

- They give you more control over what is entered in your

---

1. *A bibliographic database holds descriptions of writings and publications. These are consulted by bookshops, libraries, and some other book retailers.*

2. *An imprint is an identity under which a book is published. Usually something different to the author's name.*

book's metadata. (*The topic this book is dealing with*).

Some points you need to be aware of.

- ISBNs don't provide any legal or copyright[3] protection.

- An ISBN can only be used once. Once allocated, it remains with the book forever, even if it goes out of print. It also remains allocated to the named publisher.

- An ISBN can only be used for one format of a book: hardback, paperback, ebook, or audiobook.

- Some publishing sites will not permit you to publish the same format of your book (hardback, paperback, etc.) with the same ISBN as you've used elsewhere.

- If you make any major changes to your book, you have to use a new ISBN. For example: substantial textual changes, adding new material, change of publisher, change of title, translation into another language, publishing in a different size, change of format, and so on. You don't need a new one if your changes aren't major. For example: correcting typos, punctuation, and so on.

---

3. *Copyright is the topic of chapter 10.*

- Most bookshops, and some online retailers, will not consider stocking a book if it doesn't have an ISBN.

You now have some knowledge of what an ISBN is, what it does, and who uses them.

One bit of information to put things in a bit more context. Apparently over forty percent of ebooks sold through Amazon don't have ISBNs.

Takeaway

- An ISBN is a globally recognised identifier for a single product, a book in our case.

- Each format has to have a separate ISBN.

- Bookshops, libraries, etc. require each book to have an ISBN.

- ISBNs don't provide any copyright protection.

- There're advantages to having your own ISBN.

4

Category

Category is a broad term that refers to which group of books yours belongs. In principle, it's a high level identification such as Fiction, Non-Fiction, Children's, and so on. It helps readers know up-front if your book may be one they'd be interested in reading.

Note: Over time, the system has been manipulated to go further than the high level identification it was originally designed for. Most categories and codes now include what was previously described as a book's genre. More about those in the next chapter.

In this chapter, we'll have a look at BISACs, Amazon categories, and Thema codes. All of which are relevant to current book publishing.

BISAC is the acronym for 'Book Industry Standards and Communications'. BISACs are a classification system that determines the category for your book. These:

- Guide where your book will be placed on online retail sites, and which shelf it's placed on in a bookshop.

- Identify the subject of your book.

- Are an industry approved list of subject descriptions.

- Provide a standard subject code list that companies use to categorise books.

It's important for you to get your book placed in the correct, relevant categories. If it's not, readers will have difficulty finding it. The BISAC codes enable you to do this.

A BISAC has several parts, which make them supper helpful for publishers, retailers, and online search engines. The code helps them identify where your book belongs, and which readers are likely to be interested in it. I won't take up your time, or mine, with an unnecessarily long explanation of all the various parts. What you need to know is BISACS have various levels, which help you more readily identify your book's content. By using them, you avoid your book being filed among the millions of others within a generalised category, where it's unlikely the readers you are looking for will find it. By using a specific code, or combination of codes, you're helping your readers, and are more likely to be found.

BISAC codes have nine alphanumeric characters. For example:

HIS002020 = HISTORY/Ancient
GAR004060 = GARDENING/Flowers/Roses

You see from the last one that you can get quite specific. The codes can go down to four levels e.g. HISTORY/Ancient/Roman/Macedonian

You can now see how important and useful it is for you to ensure you select the correct, relevant category code. It can make a vast difference for your book's success or failure.

BISACs are primarily used by the North America book industry where most of the publishing systems independent authors like us use are based. As part of the process of uploading your book for publication, you'll be asked to select at least one BISAC. The systems normally provide a dropdown list for you to choose from. Most systems allow you to select three, and you're advised to take advantage of this. Provided you pick correctly, the multiple choice should help your book appear in more than one search result. Try to avoid the 'General' codes. These don't really help. It can feel frustrating when you're in a hurry to publish, to spend time trawling through the lists, but it's well worth taking the time to do so. You should be able to find more precisely defined codes for your book. If you're sure you can't, then use the 'General' one, but only as a last resort. The publisher Random House, before it became part of Penguin, had a strong selling book that had the BISAC for 'FICTION/General'. Though it was already a good seller, they decided to change the BISAC to 'FICTION/Suspense'. Sales went up by fifty-five percent! You see what a change picking a more descriptive code can make.

Note: BISACs are recognised worldwide and you may find a publishing system not based in the USA asking you to select one or more. Whenever the opportunity arises, make sure you take advantage of it.

If you'd like to see the full list of current BISAC codes before uploading your book for publishing, you can do so at:
https://www.bisg.org/complete-bisac-subject-headings-list

In the past Amazon, or rather KDP (Kindle Direct Publishing), the publishing arm of Amazon, asked authors to select three BISACs, which it then used to identify where to place your book. They no longer ask. Instead, they developed their own category lists from which you're asked to select. This was a huge change and is definitely in our favour. Current estimates (*as at the time of writing*) are that there are 3000+ BISAC codes, but 16000+ Amazon categories. That's a massive difference that enables you to drill down to very representative category codes for your books.

This creates a great advantage for readers, enabling them to find exactly what they're looking for and for you to be found. Again, it's very important you choose the right, most appropriate categories. If you don't, Amazon's systems will notice. Amazon reserves the right to place your book in the categories it considers most appropriate and, if you've entered ones that aren't relevant, it could end up somewhere you don't want or where it'll be difficult for readers to find. There's also the danger Amazon may penalise you, or even block your account, especially if you make a habit of not selecting relevant categories.

You need to be aware that Amazon splits its categories between physical books (*hardback/paperback*) and ebooks. If you're publishing in both formats, physical and digital, make sure you select the categories for both. For example:

Hardback/Paperback: books>reference>writing, research & publishing guides>publishing & books>authorship

eBook: kindle books>reference>writing, research & publishing guides>publishing & books>authorship

Though the difference is slight in the above examples, not having both (*when you're publishing in both formats*) is likely to affect where your book shows up. In addition, there are some categories, which are not included in both. Take the time to go through the lists and ensure you chose the most relevant codes from each.

Note: Amazon reserves the right to change its codes and to adjust what information it requires from authors. And it often does.

Though BISACs are recognised worldwide, they tend to only be used for the North America book industry. The rest of the world now, primarily, uses Thema codes. I say 'primarily', because until recently, most jurisdictions had their own category lists. Some still utilise them while they move over to the Thema scheme.

Thema codes provide an international standard for the global book trade. These are multilingual codes that have been translated into all languages. This makes it easier for a book's details to be shared across all jurisdictions. It also means countries can dispense with their own national subject schemes. It also makes it much easier for you, the author. Previously, if your book was to be published in a variety of different regions, you'd need to consider codes from the various national schemes. Now you only have to go to one list that's in your language but is automatically converted to other languages where appropriate.

Thema codes are mostly letter codes. For example:

CBW = Writing and editing guides

CBV = Creative writing and creative writing guides ...

In addition, there are some 'qualifier' codes. These help you identify more exactly the content of your book. These are numeric-alpha codes. For example:

5J = Subject matter intended exclusively for specific groups ...
1D = Europe (*This identifies where the action in your book takes place, thereby helping people find what they're specifically looking for.*)

There are a variety of qualifier codes for different aspects, place, language, time period, and more. These are advantageous for you, as they allow you to pinpoint your book more accurately, meaning you have a better chance of reaching the readers you want and those who'll be specifically interested in your book.

You can see a complete list of Thema codes at:
https://ns.editeur.org/thema/en

Current suggestions are that you pick four Thema codes, but no more. Too many and your book will probably not be categorised correctly.

There're some important points to note about picking your category codes.

- Only choose categories that reflect the content of your entire book. Don't pick ones that only relate to a sub-topic, theme, or chapter. You need to show what your book is about in total. If you don't, it's likely you'll find it placed in wrong, inappropriate, or irrelevant categories. Readers interested in your type of book will have difficulty finding it, or more than likely won't find it.

- Make sure you place the most relevant category, the one that best describes the content of your book, first. Some sites focus in on the first and don't bother much with the others. This applies no matter which category system you're using. It may be that the company you're using will rearrange codes into an alphanumeric order, but at least you'll have done your best to get it properly catalogued.

- With Thema codes, avoid using single letter codes. These are too general and will not help your book's visibility.

- Where you have the option, use both BISAC and Thema codes. Though BISACs are currently for the North America book industry, they're recognised worldwide and you may find some non-USA based publishing sites ask you to enter them. Despite the USA not having taken up Thema codes to a great extent, it's possible, and I would say likely, they'll consider them in the future. Save yourself time by entering them now, where you can.

Takeaway

- Whatever service you're using to publish your book, you'll need to select at least three category codes.

- Picking correct, relevant category codes is vital.

- Put the most relevant codes first.

- Avoid general codes.

- Don't choose too many.

5

Genre

Technically, genre is different to category, but as you'll see shortly, in modern times the two have tended to become synonymous. Nevertheless, there's a difference that you need to be aware of.

Authors and readers will often refer to a book as falling within a specific genre, but do they really understand what 'genre' means? Genre conveys the kind, sort, style, or form of a communication. In other words, it tells your prospective reader the type of book they're looking at. A couple of dictionary definitions may help:

'Style of art or literature.' (*Oxford English Dictionary*)

'A category of artistic, musical or literary composition characterised by a particular style, form, or content.' (*Merriam-Webster Dictionary*)

The word originates from 1770 French and meant 'kind, sort, style'. In modern usage, it principally refers to style and category.

Genre doesn't relate to the format of a book, for example, picture-book, graphic novel, paperback. Nor, though there are a few who suggest otherwise, does it identify if the book is a novel, a short story, and so on. However, with respect to the latter, you'll occasionally come across a category that includes the words 'short story'. Technically, that's the category[1], not the genre.

That brings me to the matter of category verses genre, and where the difference lies. The topic of genre verses categories can be confusing. In the past category was intended to be a broad term that referred to the general aspects of your book's content and audience, such as fiction, non-fiction, children's, young adult, and so on. Genre was then intended to be a sub-category that provided a more in depth, precise definition of what your book is about: science-fiction, crime, history, memoir, and more. In modern usage, these differences have become blurred. Category lists now drill down into far more detailed subject descriptions. In effect, they now combine category and genre into one all-encompassing code.

---

1. *Category is the topic of chapter 4.*

It's still important for you to understand, define, and state the genre your book falls into. This not only helps your readers, but may also help you pinpoint what it is you really want to write about. We sometimes have various ideas and can become a little lost.

It's accepted your book can sometimes cross more than one genre, but you should take care when submitting it for publication or listing it somewhere. Make sure you select the primary genre first. Then, if the facility provides for it, you can identify the others by choosing appropriate category codes.

Over the years, genre have become subject to change. This is usually driven by trends. As a result, there are now vast selections of sub-genre.

To give you some idea of how genre differ, I'll list a few along with dictionary definitions.

Note: The order in which the genre are presented is not indicative of any preference or suggested value of one above the other.

Fantasy:

'The imagining of improbable things.'; 'An imagined situation.'; 'Fiction involving magic or adventure.' (*Oxford English Dictionary*)

'A pleasant situation that you enjoy thinking about but is unlikely to happen, or the activity of imagining things like this.'; 'A story or type of literature that describes situations that are very different from real life, usually involving magic.' (*Cambridge Dictionary*)

Science-Fiction:

'Fiction dealing principally with the impact of actual or imagined science on society or individuals or having a scientific factor as an essential orienting component.' (*Merriam-Webster Dictionary*)

'Fiction based on imagined future scientific or technological advances and major social or environmental changes, frequently portraying space or time travel and life on other planets.' (*Oxford Dictionary*)

Romance:

'A medieval tale based on legend, chivalric love and adventure, or the supernatural.'; 'A prose narrative treating imaginary characters involved in events remote in time or place and usually heroic, adventurous, or mysterious.'; 'A love story especially in the form of a novel.' (*Merriam-Webster Dictionary*)

'A genre of fiction dealing with love in a sentimental or idealized way.' (*Oxford Dictionary*)

Thriller:

'A thriller is a book, film, or play that tells an exciting fictional story about something such as criminal activities or spying.' (*Collins Dictionary*)

'A book, film, play, etc. depicting crime, mystery, or espionage in an atmosphere of excitement and suspense.' (*The Free Dictionary*)

Mystery:

'A mystery story is a story in which strange things happen that are not explained until the end.' (*Collins Dictionary*)

'A novel, play, or film dealing with a puzzling crime, especially a murder.' (*Oxford Dictionary*)

Suspense:

'A quality in a work of fiction that arouses excited expectation or uncertainty about what may happen.' (*Oxford Dictionary*)

Note: The suspense genre is often included under, or with, Thriller (See above).

Dystopia:

'An imaginary place or state in which the condition of life is extremely bad, as from deprivation, oppression, or terror.'; 'A work describing such a place or state.'; 'An imaginary society in which social or technological trends have culminated in a greatly diminished quality of life or degradation of values.' (*The Free Dictionary*)

'An imagined state or society in which there is great suffering or injustice, typically one that is totalitarian or post-apocalyptic.' (*Oxford Dictionary*)

Biography:

'A biography of someone is an account of their life, written by someone else.'; 'Biography is the branch of literature which deals with accounts of people's lives.' (*Collins Dictionary*)

'An account of a person's life written, composed, or produced by another.' (*The Free Dictionary*)

Autobiography:

'The story of a person's life written by that person.' (*Oxford English Dictionary*)

'The biography of a person narrated by himself or herself.' (*Merriam-Webster Dictionary*)

Memoir:

'A written account of events etc. that you remember.' (*Oxford English Dictionary*)

'A narrative composed from personal experience.' (*Merriam-Webster Dictionary*)

You'll appreciate there are far more genre and sub-genre than those mentioned above.

Takeaway

- There's a difference between genre and category.
- Genre defines more specifically what your book is about.
- Modern category codes tend to incorporate genre as well.
- Ensure you're clear about which genre your book primarily falls into.

6

KEYWORDS

Keywords are words (*individual or a combination*) or short phrases that describe the content of your book. They're a vital part of your book's metadata because, as you'll see in a moment, they also guide the placing of your book. My aim here is to provide you with an overview of what keywords are to help you understand how they fit into the metadata of your book. This is not an in-depth look at the topic. I will, however, include a few hints for how to choose appropriate ones.

A keyword is essentially what a reader is likely to enter in a search bar when searching for their next read. This usually refers to a specific topic, genre, or sub-genre. For example, if they're looking for a romance set within a western, they may enter 'cowboy romance'. If they're looking for a mystery that's not too graphic or horror filled, they may enter 'cosy mystery'. You get the idea.

Another very important keyword usage to note is that search engines use them extensively. You see, therefore, it's important to pick the right keywords for your book. A keyword should describe the content of your book, at least part of the content. You'll have the option to use several keywords, which combined should provide a comprehensive insight into what your book is about. The number of keywords you can use for your book depends on the publishing system you choose. There's no restriction on how many you'll use for your publicity and marketing. If you're not using them for those, you need to start. Search engines scour the whole of the internet, not just publisher or book retailer sites.

It's not easy to always find the correct keyword selection for your book. To start, consider your book's category[1], sub-category (*genre*)[2], topic, theme, setting, time period, characters, character traits, and so on. You should also study the ones other authors in your genre use for their books. List as many as you can think of, or have discovered. These will act as your basis for keywords, which you may then refine. Ultimately, you should end up with at least seven keywords (*individual words, combinations of words, or phrases*) to include with your book's metadata.

---

1. *Category is the topic of chapter 4.*

2. *Genre is the topic of chapter 5.*

Two things to be careful with:

1. The keywords you choose must be relevant to the actual content of your book, and must reflect the category you believe your book falls in. Failure to do this will lead to disappointment for your readers and, more importantly, may lead to the retailer placing your book in categories you don't want. Some think having your book in multiple categories, whether relevant or not, will lead to greater exposure. In fact, this is usually counter-productive, because readers will soon detect what they're likely to consider spamming behaviour (*the sending of unsolicited material or information*) with the consequent results.

2. The order in which you enter words within a keyword, *where there's more than one word*. Most times this will be the situation. Kindle Direct Publishing (KDP), the publishing arm of Amazon, provides the following as an example. They suggest readers are likely to search for 'military science fiction' but not 'fiction science military'. This may appear a subtle difference, but it really matters because the search system is likely to look for the combined order of words rather than the individual words. If it looked at each word, all sorts of irrelevant results will be sent back. That wouldn't help the reader, and they're likely to give up looking.

If you're unsure if a keyword is appropriate for your book, and sometimes even if you're sure, it helps to enter it in your system search bar and see what comes back. Sometimes what you think is ideal can turn out to be less than you hope. You should also think about your readers, or the readers you hope to attract. What word or phrase are they likely to enter for their search? Bear in mind, despite what you may think, your book is not for everyone. There's no such thing as a book for everyone. We're all different and have varied outlooks. Even if our reading falls within the same genre as others, it may be at a different angle. One romance reader may prefer one set in Georgian England, whereas another will prefer one set on a space station. You need to think carefully of where in the range of categories and sub-categories your book falls.

Takeaway

- Keywords may be a single word, a combination of words, or a short phrase.

- Keywords must be relevant to the content of your book.

- Search engines use keywords to find relevant information to send back to a searcher.

- Publishing systems use them to identify the category your book belongs in.

- The order in which you put the words in a keyword can make or break its success.

7

Blurb

If you're a new author, the word 'Blurb' may appear strange. A Blurb is a brief, catchy description of your book. In some places, you'll see it described as 'book description'. I've opted to use 'Blurb' because it's the term used most widely. You'll sometimes see people refer to these descriptions as a synopsis. They are not the same. A synopsis is a far different product. Though brief, it goes into far more detail that covers the plot, the action, and the ending, or for non-fiction, the topics, style, and conclusions. Not something you'd want readers to see upfront. If they did, why would they bother buying your book? You'll only use a synopsis where you're submitting your book to a traditional publisher, or sometimes an editor. A synopsis does not form part of your book's metadata. I'll therefore not be discussing them further in this guide.

Many authors will tell you writing the blurb is often far more challenging than writing the book. That's because you're trying to present a captivating overview of your complete book in a few words and with no spoilers (*giving an important element or the end away*). No simple task when you want to keep within 150-200 words.

Blurbs are used for online book pages, marketing, publicity, the back of a physical book, search engines (*these will see the words and may provide results based upon them*), bookshops and libraries (*if you're lucky enough to have your book in one of them*), and book list services (*primarily those that record ISBNs[1]*).

A blurb can impact how well your book will sell or not.

Three points to help when thinking of how to write and phrase your blurb:

1. Think from the reader's perspective. Why should they bother reading this book? What's in it for them?

2. What words or phrases would someone enter in a search when looking for a book like yours?

3. Use simple, straightforward words and language. Don't try to appear clever by using complicated, highbrow terminology. You'll lose most readers straight away. I mean, they'll move on within seconds.

---

1. *ISBNs are the topic of chapter 3.*

The content and format of a blurb differs for fiction and non-fiction. To start, I'll consider blurbs for fiction. If you're writing non-fiction, you may prefer to skip to further on in the chapter. Though you may find parts of the information in both will help you, irrespective of your book type.

Blurbs for Fiction

Your blurb should be enticing and full of intrigue. The idea is to catch a prospective reader's attention and hold it so they go on to consider buying your book. An important point to bear in mind throughout, is people don't really read online. They scan. If something doesn't immediately catch their attention, they'll move on, usually within seconds. Therefore, you should do your utmost to make the first sentence as captivating as possible, so it encourages them to read the rest of the description.

Ensure you give some indication as to the nature (genre[2]) of your book. Reader's need to know it's something they'll be interested in. You don't want a romance reader picking up your science-fiction story. That'll more than likely result in a critical review or worse.

---

2. *Genre is the topic of chapter 5.*

Naming your primary character and describing, without giving anything vital away, the journey they're about to take is a good place to start. Your aim is to get the reader emotionally involved so they'll want more. If you can also get them to sympathise with your character, even better. You could do this by indicating what the character has to lose if they don't achieve, or reach, their goal. All these will help your reader know what the book is about. How often have you looked for your next read but been put off when there's little information about the story?

If they've an important part in your story, you could include something about the setting or time period in which your story is set. Some readers are specifically interested in books linked to certain locations or historical events or periods. Similarly, if your story is set in a fictional world, like a mystical or science fiction setting, you should clearly point that out.

If your book covers a specific topic or theme, such as women, travel, family, and so on, it'll help your prospective reader if you include a reference to it within your blurb.

I think the above gives you an idea of the sort of things you can include in your blurb. As I said at the start, blurbs are hard to write. You'll probably spend a lot more time and effort than you'd expect. Your blurb can also help you, as it makes you focus on the essence of your story and may even highlight where something doesn't work.

Try to include relevant keywords[3]. These will also help the reader identify if it's a book they'd be interested in reading. Remember, no book is for everyone, even if you think it should be. That's unrealistic and can easily backfire. There'll be readers for your book and you need to focus your description toward them.

It may help if you can see your blurb as a visual trailer that highlights important, intriguing moments without giving the story or crucial action away. You're probably used to seeing these for television and film productions. Watch them and see what points and words they highlight.

The format of your blurb is also something you need to think about. Remember, you are trying to capture a reader's attention within a few initial seconds.

You'd be wise to start with a single captivating sentence. This could be in bold text. Many book retail sites initially only show the first part of a blurb. The reader sometimes has to click to see the rest. This sentence is therefore a vital component of your blurb. Also, as I previously mentioned, online readers scan rather than read word for word. You need to catch their attention quickly.

---

3. *Keywords are the topic of chapter 6.*

The rest of your blurb should be made up of short paragraphs. Large blocks of text are an off putter when people are flicking through online pages. Unless you've captured their attention, they'll quickly move on.

You may find it helps to look at the blurbs for other books similar to your own, or books within the same genre. You could also look at any reviews of those books, which may give you an idea of what readers look for in a story. Some suggest also including a reference to comparative books that will encourage the reader to pick up your book if they liked the ones you reference. If you do this, make sure your book really does fall within the same style, type, and genre.

You'll come across varied advice for how to end your blurb. Some suggest ending with a cliffhanger that leaves your readers wanting to know what happens. Others suggest, I would say the majority, you end with a call-to-action (CTA). In other words, something that encourages the reader to buy your book there and then. The choice is yours, but make sure you're comfortable with it and it's aimed at achieving what you want.

Blurbs for Non-Fiction

Most non-fiction books aim to provide solutions, or help, with something the reader wants to solve. You need to highlight the problem you're aiming to solve and give some idea of how your book will do this. Be careful not to give all your solutions away, otherwise there'll be no need for them to buy your book. Including some relevant keywords will help.

If possible, include a brief explanation of what qualifies you to write the book. Highlight your experience, how you gained the knowledge, and more. This will provide the reader with confidence that you know, and understand, what you're talking about.

The formatting of a non-fiction blurb is different to that for fiction. You're still trying to capture prospective readers' attentions, but those looking for a book like yours tend to have a different focus.

As with all blurbs, you'll need to start with a clear, captivating first sentence. You should put this in bold text, but not necessarily uppercase. That can sometimes appear unprofessional. And, again, remember, with online sites, it's often only the first part of your blurb that is shown upfront.

Unlike blurbs for fiction, where you should stick to simple, plain text and short paragraphs, with non-fiction ones you should consider using larger fonts, bold, underlining, and lists. The paragraphs should still be short but occasionally interspersed with single sentence statements in bold that highlight the most important points. But, be careful not to overdo it. You'll want the blurb to look professional and be easy for the reader's eye to follow. Overuse can diminish the impact and may put some readers off.

Lists are great for explaining what the reader can hope to gain from your book. List some of the things they'll learn. Suggestion is you make this personal by stating 'you'll learn', rather than just listing the subjects. For example, I could use the following for this book:

'In this detailed guide, you'll learn:

- What metadata is and how it impacts your book sales.
- The different types of metadata.
- How to prepare and format your book's metadata.'

You could also include a list of what your book covers:

'You'll find information and guidance for your:

- Copyright
- Blurb
- Categories

- Keywords

- And a Lot More.'

You get the idea.

With non-fiction, the general consensus is to end with a CTA.

'**BUY NOW** to get your metadata into the best possible order quickly.'

I admit I'm not found of such outright 'buy' CTAs, but research indicates many readers need such a prompt to get them taking action.

Takeaway

- Your blurb should be between 150-200 words. (*Anything longer and the reader may move away.*)

- Ensure the first sentence is captivating.

- Keep it simple and clear.

- Include some relevant keywords.

- End with a call-to-action or cliffhanger.

8

AGE & GRADE

You'll frequently see this section of your metadata described as 'Primary audience'.

When you upload or submit your book to a publishing system, or publisher, you're usually asked to identify if it's an adult only book or one for younger readers.

Note: As most online publishing systems are based in the United States, they generally use American terminology.

It's crucial you identify whether your book contains explicit sexual, violent, or horrific content. If it does, and you don't, you'll find yourself in trouble. Your book will probably be withdrawn and you'll be banned. Though this is primarily for the protection of children, there are also adult readers who don't want such books. Should your book somehow get through the system, complaints and very negative reviews will soon bring it to the attention of those monitoring the quality and accuracy of books. Failing to identify such content will also result in you gaining a bad reputation that'll quickly spread. Most readers will subsequently avoid anything you've written, even if it doesn't contain similar material.

KDP (Kindle Direct Publishing), the publishing arm of Amazon, asks you to tick a box next to their question of whether your book contains sexually explicit images or title. Though not stated in the question, this also includes sexually related language, which they clarify in the guidance notes. You MUST tick the 'Yes' box if it applies. If you don't, you'll suffer the same consequences as outlined in the previous paragraph.

If your book is for young people, some sites will ask you to identify the age range. This may either be by stating the age group or the grade. Grade relates to the American school system. At the time of writing, this is:

Preschool - ages 2 to 5
Elementary School - ages 5 to 10 (Covers grades 1 - 5)
Middle School - ages 11 to 13 (Covers grades 6 - 8)
High School - ages 14 to 18 (Covers grades 9 - 12)

KDP, as with many of Amazon's functions, uses its own system:

Ages 0 to 2 - Simple Picture Books with few or no words.

Ages 3 to 5 - Picture Books.
Ages 6 to 8 - Early-level readers, first chapter books.
Ages 9 to 12 - Middle-grade chapter books.
Ages 13 to 17 - Teen and young adult chapter books.

You'll note, even with these, American school grades are either implied or referenced.

As part of your book's metadata, age and grade can help readers find your book. Getting it right will ensure you hit the right reader group. Get it wrong and you'll pay the price.

Takeaway

- It's vital you identify if your book contains any sexual, violent, or horrific material.

- If your book is for younger readers, you need to identify your target age range.

- Double check you've entered the correct information.

- You'll pay the price if you enter incorrect information, or try to trick the systems.

9

Contributors

A contributor is someone who's been involved with the creation of your book. They're people who've 'contributed' their ideas and skills to making your book what it is. You need to have it clear in your mind that these differ from those who've helped you along the line with encouragement and support. Second authors, ghostwriters, editors, illustrators, narrators (*where you've been able to afford an audiobook edition*), translators (*if you've chosen to make your book available in other languages*), and so on are all considered contributors to your book. We'll have a closer look at some of those.

Second authors: You'll sometimes see these referred to as a co-author, but that's an inaccurate description. A co-author is someone you've combined with to write the whole of your book. Co-authors have the same status as you. They'll be listed along with you as joint author, on the book cover and everywhere the author's name is shown. A second author is someone who's only contributed some of your book's content. They may be described as a 'contributing author', but their name will not appear next to yours on the cover or elsewhere. You, however, have responsibility for giving them their due credit.

Ghostwriters: (*Someone who writes a book for someone else, in that person's name.*) People use ghostwriters for a variety of reasons, such as, they don't enjoy writing, they don't think they're a good writer, they don't have time to write a book, and more. The ghostwriter undertakes the task for them either working from conversations and interviews or from notes provided to them. They always stay in the background. You, the author, are under no obligation to name them. In my personal opinion, I consider that to be mean-spirited. Some who've chosen to do so, identify them in a variety of ways: co-author, writer, editor, person who typed my book, and others. I don't see why they can't be identified as the 'ghostwriter.' After all, they're a major contributor to the creation of your book. Without them, it'd probably never have seen the light of day.

Editors: (*Someone who checks the words, grammar, punctuation, story flow, and more of a book.*) Editing is a complex subject because of the various types of editing. That's a topic for a different guide. An industry insider stated some years ago an author should not automatically credit an editor. They should first ask if the editor wishes to be named. Apparently there can be issues round this, meaning some editors prefer to remain out of sight. This is usually due to it being their personal policy rather than for any negative reasons. There's no compulsion for you to acknowledge your editor and in the end it will be entirely at their or your, if they agree, choice. All this is on the assumption you've employed an editor, but the truth is most independent authors can't afford one. A lot of attention and time is involved in editing and they deserve their fee, but it's often out of reach of the ordinary independent author.

Narrators: ACX (Amazon's audiobook publishing site) insists, along with the title and author, the narrator is named in the opening credits of an audiobook. That, to me, seems only fair. Narrating a book is no easy task and takes many hours of work, and often re-recording. To say they are a major contributor to your audiobook's existence is no exaggeration. The same applies whatever audio publisher or system you use.

Translators: Whether the translator's name appears on the cover of your book is entirely the publisher's choice. As an independent author, that's you. I've never had a book translated and therefore am not in a position to offer any advice. I know a translator's name usually appears on the copyright[1] page of your book. Again, translation is an arduous task. It takes time and considerable attention because it's not just a straightforward translation of word

---

1. *Copyright is the topic of chapter 10.*

for word. The language's grammar, generally accepted style, and idiosyncrasies have to be taken into account. With some languages, there's also the different script. Japanese and arabica for example. A translator deserves recognition.

As you've now seen, a contributor adds something tangible to your book. They are different from those who support you through the writing and publishing processes. Those are normally family and friends. Obviously, there's no reason someone can't fulfil both roles. To be of value to your book's metadata, a contributor has to be named, but, as we have seen, not all are.

You may already be aware many books include an 'Acknowledgments' section in which the author thanks all those who've helped them along the way. Some authors choose to include contributors in that section and there's nothing wrong with doing that. You also have the option of adding a further 'Contributors' section. This makes clear who has materially helped your book come into existence and, again in my personal opinion, provides them with more visible direct appreciation and recognition. The choice is entirely yours. So is whether to include a short bio (biography) for the contributor, as some suggest. Many authors don't.

As I've said, I consider it fair and right, and good manners, to name those who've helped bring your book into existence. That's as long as they agree. You'd be wise to check because some have good reason for not wanting their name published. Besides, giving the contributor due credit, including their details may also bring you and your book further exposure. Readers who know and like the person, having come across their name in books they've read, may also search for other books they've been involved with. If you've not bothered to credit the person, your book has little chance of being found by those readers. I stress this isn't the reason to name and thank the contributor. You should be doing that out of appreciation, nothing else.

Takeaway

- There're many people who can contribute to your book coming into existence.

- A contributor deserves recognition, even if there's no obligation for you to name them, but ask first.

- A contributor is different to someone how supports you through the writing and publishing processes.

- Some publishing sites insist you name a contributor. ACX for example.

10

COPYRIGHT

Copyright is the legal ownership of intellectual property. That, for you, is your book, or more accurately, your manuscript. Copyright law recognises the exclusive legal right you have to publish, sell, and reproduce work you've created, your book for example. It protects your work for a specified period and stops others from using it without your permission.

Copyright is granted automatically from the moment you create an original work. In our case, that'd be a text document, such as your manuscript. You don't have to apply for copyright. As said, it's automatic. Nor do you have to pay for it. Don't get taken in by sites or companies that offer copyright protection for a fee. They've no legal standing in the protection of copyright. Note the word 'create', copyright does NOT protect the idea or information behind your work. It's only the work itself that benefits. Names and titles are not covered by copyright, nor are book covers.

Copyright prevents people from using your work without your permission. It stops them: copying it, giving out copies (*for free or at a price*), renting or lending copies, performing, showing, or playing it in public (*a public reading for instance*), making an adaption, or placing it on the internet.

Note: Copyright doesn't stop secondhand books shops selling used copies of your book. I hope you wouldn't want it to.

You need to know there are some exceptions to the above restraints, usually identified as 'Fair Dealing' or 'Fair Use'. This allows limited parts of your book to be used for non-commercial research, private study, criticism, reviews, reporting current events, legal proceedings, and teaching. Limited parts of your work may also be used for parody, caricature, and pastiche (*something that imitates your style and work*). Such use is allowed on the provision that it doesn't impact the market for your original work, and doesn't cause you to lose revenue. You should note the emphasis on 'limited'. Should an accusation of misuse arise, the court will consider whether the amount used is 'reasonable and appropriate'. A further exception to be aware of is that some organisations and charities are permitted to make copies of the whole of your book for use by disabled people. For example, they can have it converted into brail, audio, or large print. There's no actual legal definition of fair dealing, or reasonable and appropriate. Each situation is judged on its own merits. The explanations given here are those courts have considered in cases brought before them.

Included in your copyright are two other rights: economic rights and moral rights.

Economic rights give you the right to make commercial gain from your work, money in other words. Obviously, selling your book falls within this, but it also recognises your right to licence others to use your work, or to sell your rights. You can make a gift of both, but in most instances you'll be asking for a payment.

Moral rights are your non-commercial rights:

- You've the right to be recognised as the author of your book. To benefit from this, you've to assert your right to be identified as such. You can do that with a specific statement, as I explain in a moment.

- You can object to any negative use of your book. This applies to anything that distorts it, whether by adding, deleting, or altering something. It also includes anything that may reflect negatively on your reputation as an author.

- You may also object to someone trying to name you as the author of a work you didn't create.

You'll appreciate I'm primarily providing you with an overview, though I consider it covers the important details. If you wish to delve further, you should research the copyright laws for whichever country or state you live in.

In most books you'll usually see, within the first couple of pages, the word 'Copyright' followed by a © (*the recognised copyright symbol*), a year, and a name. The year is the one in which you created the content for your book. Most times, this is the same year in which you publish it, but not necessarily. It's at the point of creation copyright is applied. Statements, asserting your right to be identified as the author, and expanding upon the rights you hold, normally follow. You can see an example on the copyright page at the front of this book. This one relates to UK law, you'll need to research equivalent law for your jurisdiction. The copyright word, symbol and statement are not a legal requirement. Even when not shown, copyright is still applied. To avoid any possible confusion, and to make matters clear for your readers, you're advised to include each in any book you publish. Just a point about the copyright statement. There are various forms. It's up to you which, if any, you use. Most publishing sites have suggestions. Some works just have the symbol, year, and name. The name is obviously your author name, whether it's your real name or a pen name. You still have protection when using a pen name.

Earlier I mentioned you can licence your work for a fee, however, there is another type of licence called an 'implied licence'. This is when there's nothing in writing or there's been no verbal agreement, and yet there're indications the copyright owner, you, expected your work to be used in the way you foresaw. The following rarely arises, but if you've been in the habit of allowing someone to use your work without entering into a contract, and then change your mind, a court will probably consider, by your previous actions, the person using your work had a reasonable expectation to consider they'd an implied licence to use it.

You may be thinking about what protection your book has if it's sold in another country. No need to worry. There're various treaties to cover you. The best known is the Berne Convention for the Protection of Literary and Artistic Works. Most countries have signed up to it. To be a member of the convention, each country must have copyright laws in place. You're granted protection under those laws. In most cases these protections are very similar to the ones you have in your own country or state.

Copyright isn't granted forever. There are various time limits depending on the type of work. In general, the period for books is the author's lifetime plus seventy years. After that, the book falls into what is called the 'public domain', meaning anyone is free to use it without risk of penalty.

Unfortunately, most countries don't have a formal registry for copyright. This can pose a problem if someone plagiarises (*copying and saying someone else's work is your own*), or misuses your book. To prove the point, you'll usually need to take them to court. There're suggested ways to try and have the means to prove your book is yours, but they're not foolproof. The main alternatives are to deposit a copy of your work with a bank or solicitor, or to use what is often referred to as 'The poor man's copyright'. That is where you send yourself a copy by registered post. You then keep it safe, <u>unopened</u>. The postmark must be clear because the date and time will be important in any action brought. The envelope has to be presented intact. If it's damaged in any way, the court is unlikely to accept it as proof. You should be aware, once the envelope has been opened, it can no longer be used as proof of copyright.

The truth is, most of us can't afford the costs of a court case. It's frustrating. If your work is pirated, try looking on the positive side. At least your book is gaining further exposure. You may not be paid, but it could result in readers becoming aware of your work and looking for other books you've written.

Though copyright laws in most countries are very similar there can be some differences. To give you an idea, I'll highlight a couple. In Australia, copyright doesn't prevent someone else from independently publishing the same work. I find that strange, because as far as I can see, that would be considered an infringement elsewhere. In the USA, the date at when copyright expires can vary. It depends on which state the author is in. Some states follow the usual copyright duration of the author's life plus seventy years, while others apply seventy years from the date of publication. Those are just examples. If you've any concerns, you'd be best reading the copyright legislation for the country or state you're concerned about.

Takeaway:

- Copyright is granted automatically from the moment the original work is created.

- Copyright doesn't last forever. There are time limits, most commonly the authors' life plus seventy years.

- Authors are advised to include a copyright statement in their books.

11

PRICE

Pricing your book can be tricky.

You'll need to consider a variety of things before deciding on a price. You'll also have to take into account the varied costs for producing your book, especially between print and digital (ebooks).

Though you'll want to make your book attractive for potential readers, you'll also want to earn some money (*commonly known as your royalty*). That, however, may depend upon your overall aim at the time of publishing (*your aims can change over time*). For example, do you just want to get as much money as you can, or do you wish to get readers to like your books and follow you, or do you need to cover production costs? Maybe a combination. Whatever your aim, you'll need to consider how it impacts your pricing choice.

With your pricing, you're telling readers what you think your book, and the work you put into it is worth. But, be realistic. Readers who find your book will weigh it against similar books by authors they already know and trust. Overpricing will make them less willing to chance their hard earned cash with you, the unknown. Similarly, underpricing may lead them to conclude your book can't be as good as the ones they know. How often has the thought crossed your mind that 'You get what you pay for.'? A product's price, whatever it is, has a psychological impact. It may be subconscious, but it's always there.

To gain attention, you might be tempted to set a very low price for your book. That has worked for some authors, but it also has its drawbacks. First, by undervaluing your book, you may, as stated above, be giving readers the impression it's not very good. Second, you'll be undervaluing your own time and effort. Third, some people will only buy your book because it's cheap. Some of those can be problematic people, who rarely provide sensible reviews, or don't bother to write a review.

Note: Many readers are too nervous to write a review. Don't expect the number of reviews to match the number of books sold. In fact, you can anticipate it being a very small percentage.

To help you hit the right price bracket, I'll explain some factors that'll impact your pricing, and some things you should consider:

- Genre can affect the market price of your book. Look at other books in your genre and note the average price readers are paying.

- Find books of a similar length, even if in a different genre, and see what the typical price range is.

- It may also help to note promotions, offers, and deductions. These can affect the price a reader is willing to pay and may make them unwilling to pay more.

- Your book type can also have an influence. Non-fiction books often fetch a higher price than fiction.

- Production costs between print and digital (ebooks) are very different. An ebook that you've uploaded yourself to a publishing system, other than the fee the company takes for their services, has little, if any, other costs, except for your time and effort. With print books, you'll have to account for the cost of paper, printing, and binding (paperback and hardback), as well as the firm's fee.

Note: Owners of publishing systems deserve their fee. Most don't charge you for uploading your book and provide a dedicated webpage for it. They are effectively marketing your book by showing it to people looking for their next read. They also have to cover delivery costs, whether that's digital or physical. Don't begrudge them earning a little. After all, they're a business, just like you are.

- You'll also need to account for any additional expenditure. For example, a cover designer, an editor, writing software fees, and so on.

You'll find a lot of advice regarding actual price brackets on the internet. I'm not going to quote any prices because they inevitably change overtime either due to rising costs or trends. I want this guide to remain useful without constantly needing to publish updates.

As mentioned above, considering your genre is important when deciding a price. You might be tempted to price your book lower than other books in it. That, however, could backfire. Readers are not only accustomed to paying within a defined price range, but expect a book to be priced within that range. A price outside that range will draw attention, though it may not be the sort of attention you want. It could raise doubts in the reader's mind, who may consequently decide to bypass it. The only exception would be if you're putting your book on offer for a short period. You'd need to make clear it's a limited time offer.

Takeaway

- Decide what's more important to you at the point of publishing, making money or developing a reader base.

- Check the price range for your genre.

- Don't over or under price.

- For print books, take into account printing and binding costs.

- Include a proportion for any other expenditure you wish to recoup.

12

AUTHOR BIO

Author Bio is often, more frequently I'd say, known as 'About the Author'. 'Bio' stands for biography, however, this is not the place for your life history.

Your aim here is to share information about yourself that:

- you think the reader should know and may be interested in;

- provides evidence of why you're the person to write this book, such as formal qualifications, awards, experience, and more;

- reveals your humanity, who you are as a person.

As with most information you publish online, you'll want to start with a short, catchy sentence that says something about you as an author. Remember, most people, you as well I suspect, scan digital content rather than read it word for word.

You'd then want to share your experience and, if relevant, any qualifications you have. Qualifications, awards, and areas of expertise are important for non-fiction. Make sure not to boast about your achievements, but simply state the facts. Most people don't like a bragger.

After, add a little personal touch. Something about where you live, your lifestyle, any appropriate hobbies. Whatever you feel comfortable with. There's no requirement for you to share details you'd rather keep private.

To finish, several suggest adding a call-to-action. Something to prompt your reader to buy one of your other books, to signup for your newsletter (*if you have one*), to leave a review, and so on. How forceful you make it is up to you. I'm not entirely convinced about a hard call-to-action. Personally, I don't tend to adopt this. I prefer finishing with something more personal. The reader may look at the 'Also by ...' page (*that's where you list your other books, if you've published any*), if they'd like to read more of your books. I must, however, point out many who provide training for authors, and experienced authors, consider a call-to-action is a must. I think this is because you can use your bio in many places besides your book, including your website, social media, publicity materials, and more. As with most things, the choice is yours.

By adding information about yourself, you'll likely to:

- build trust;

- confirm what you've got to say is worth reading;

- inspire the reader to think the book is for them; and

- help them relate to you as a person. (*Despite the fast progress of human automatons through artificial intelligence, most people still prefer to connect with another human.*)

As stated at the start, this is not the place to share your life story. This bio should be a brief overview of who you are as an author and person, and should provide confidence of why you're the right person to have written the book. With non-fiction, the last point will be easy for you to prove. It may be a little more tricky for fiction, but that's where you could provide some glimpses into your personality.

You should always write your bio in the 3rd person (he/she/his/hers/them/their/they). It's the industry standard. It also provides a little more freedom to share details without it sounding as if you're bragging.

Brevity is important. Some suggest your bio should be under three hundred words. Others state it should be no more than sixty to ninety words. I think it depends upon what it is you want to say and how well you know your readers. One hundred to one hundred and fifty words seems the ideal to me. You should certainly not exceed three hundred words.

As part of your book's metadata, search engines will scour through the words and pick up on anything that appears relevant to a search enquiry. It's therefore wise for you to read and reread your bio to ensure you've included anything that's relevant to your book. That way, it's more likely to show up in search results that, hopefully, lead to sales.

Takeaway

- Keep your bio short.
- Include things your reader could do with knowing.
- State your experience and add any qualifications or awards.
- Show your personality.
- Write in the 3rd person.

Metadata Checklist

I've created a checklist to help you with your book's metadata.

You can get your free, user-friendly copy at:
https://acauthorguides.com
It's under the 'Resources' tab.

Copyright © Adam Cartwright

To give you an idea of what it contains,
I've included a reduced copy on the next two pages.

Topic	Guidance	✓ When Completed
Title	Ensure you've done your research to find the most unique and appropriate title you can. *Enter it EXACTLY as it is to appear on all formats and in all places your book is to be displayed.*	
Sub-Title	If you're adding a sub-title, enter it in the sub-title field NOT with the primary title.	
ISBN	When using your own ISBN, make sure to enter it in the format required. Usually with the dashes (-) included. *Ensure you enter it correctly. You CAN'T change it after you've submitted your book.*	
Category (BISAC, Thema, Amazon)	Make sure you pick the right codes for your book. That's the ones that reflect the actual content.	
Genre	Most systems don't have a separate field for genre because these are now generally incorporated within categories.	
Keywords	Make sure you've done your research. *Ensure you only use keywords which reflect the content of your book.*	
Blurb	Try to keep this to 150-200 words. *Ensure the first sentence catches both the eye and the interest.*	
Age & Grade *Also known as 'Primary audience'.*	It's vital you identify if your book contains sexual content. Where your book is for younger readers, you need to enter the relevant age range or American school grade.	
Contributors	Give credit where it's due, *provided the person concerned agrees.*	
Copyright	Though it's not a legal requirement in all jurisdictions, you're advised to always include a copyright statement.	
Price	Ensure you've done your research. If you're publishing a print book, take into account printing, paper, and binding costs. (*Systems will show you the cost.*)	

Copyright © Adam Cartwright

Topic	Guidance	✓ When Completed
Author Bio	Share information that helps the reader know why you're the one to write this book. *Keep it short. 100-150 words is best, but no more than 300.*	
Series	If your book is part of a series, there'll be a field for you to enter the series title, name, or description.	
Language	Select the language your book is written in. *This helps the systems place your book on appropriate retail sites.*	
Trim Size	That's the height and width. Make sure you choose correctly as it effects the book cover template you'll need to complete.	
Sales Territory	If not preset, you'll have to identify the primary retail territory you want your book sold in. *This doesn't limit your book to that territory.*	
Publication Date	Make sure, *before you start the publishing process,* you know when you want your book to be available for purchase.	

copyright © Adam Cartwright

Finally: Ensure you <u>double check</u> all the information you enter. It's not easy to change it later and, if you have to, it often means your book has to be pulled from sale and then re-submitted.

Copyright © Adam Cartwright

ABOUT THE AUTHOR

Adam Cartwright loves to see ideas and topics turn into valuable books. He has worked as a ghostwriter, shown some how to collate their thoughts, concepts, or topic ideas into logical sequence, and assisted others in getting their manuscripts into publishing condition. In the process, and in talking with aspiring authors, Adam came to realise many struggle with the basics of the author craft. He therefore set out to provide elementary, simple to follow guides to help them fulfil their dream.

Adam enjoys seeing words take form in an entertaining or informative manner, listening to story ideas and helping them come into being, and assisting aspiring authors on the path of their creativity.

ALSO BY ADAM CARTWRIGHT

An Elementary Author Guide To: Planning A Book
An Elementary Author Guide To: Business Plans
View at:
https://acauthorguides.com
and
https://anickto.com

More to come.

Acronyms

An acronym is a word made from the first letters of other words. The book industry uses many. Definitions for those I use or refer to in this book are below.

ACX - Though this appears to be an acronym, it's not. I've included it here because I'm certain many of you will think it is, just as I did before I researched it. ACX is the name of the audio production service owned by Audible, an Amazon company.

ASIN - Amazon Standard Identification Number

BISAC - Book Industry Standards and Communications

CTA - Call-to-Action

KDP - Kindle Direct Publishing

ISBN - International Standard Book Number

Index

Some chapters cover more than one related topic. I've therefore provided this index to help you find the content or reference for any topic you're specifically interested in.

Next to the topic you'll see the chapter numbers that contain details or reference to the topic.

ACX - 9
Acknowledgments - 9
Age - 8
Also by - 12
Amazon - 2, 4
ASIN - 3
Audiobook - 3
Author Bio - 12
Autobiography - 5
Berne Convention - 10
Binding - 11

Biography - 5

BISAC - 4

Blurb - 7

Categories - 1, 4, 5, 6

Call-to-Action - 7, 12

Co-Author - 9

Codes - 4, 5

Contributor - 9

Copyright - 10

Dystopia - 5

Ebook - 3, 4, 11

Economic Rights - 10

Editor - 9

Fantasy - 5

Fair dealing - 10

Fair use - 10

Free writing - 2

Genre - 1, 2, 4, 5, 6, 7, 11

Ghostwriter - 9

Grade - 8

Hardback - 3, 4, 11

ISBN - 3

Illustrator - 9

Imprint - 3

KDP - 4, 6, 8

Keywords - 1, 2, 6, 7

Licence - 10
Memoir - 2, 5
Moral Rights - 10
Mystery - 5
Narrator - 9
Nilesen - 3
Paperback - 3, 4, 11
Price - 11
Printing - 11
Romance - 5
Royalty - 11
R. R. Bowker - 3
Science-fiction - 5
Search engines - 1, 2, 4, 6, 7, 12
Second authors - 9
Subtitle - 2
Suspence - 5
Synopsis - 7
Tax - 3
Thema - 4
Thriller - 5
Title - 2
Translators - 9

www.ingramcontent.com/pod-product-compliance
Lightning Source LLC
Chambersburg PA
CBHW031309060426
42444CB00033B/1095